TRAILBLAZING WOMEN IN
CYCLING

BY LIBBY WILSON

NORWOOD HOUSE PRESS

Cover: Marianne Vos of the Netherlands breaks away from the pack in the last kilometers of the women's road race at the 2012 World Championships in the Netherlands.

Norwood House Press

For information regarding Norwood House Press, please visit our website at: www.norwoodhousepress.com or call 866-565-2900.

Credits
Editor: Patrick Donnelly
Designer: Becky Daum
Fact Checker: Lillian Dondero

PHOTO CREDITS: Cover: © Bas Czerwinski/ANP/AP Images; © Alfred S. Campbell/Library of Congress, 5; © Danny Lawson/ EMPPL PA Wire/AP Images, 7; © The Referee & Cycle Trade Journal/Referee Publishing Company/Smithsonian Libraries and Archives, 9; © Boston Sunday Post, 10; © Kaca Skokanova/Shutterstock Images, 13; © Lorenz J. Finison, 14; © Jac. De Nijs/Dutch National Archives/Anefo/Wikimedia, 16; © Ron Kroon/Dutch National Archives/Anefo/Wikimedia, 18; © Brian Townsley/W, 21; © Italfoto/Splash News/Newscom, 23, 24, 27, 29; © Stefano Rellandini/Pool Reuters/AP Images, 31; © Christophe Ena/AP Images, 32; © Luca Bruno/AP Images, 34; © Peter Dejong/AP Images, 37; © Emilio Morenatti/AP Images, 39, 40; © Dmitry Lovetsky/AP Images, 43; © Michael Steele/Pool Getty Images/AP Images, 45

Library of Congress Cataloging-in-Publication Data
Names: Wilson, Libby, author.
Title: Trailblazing women in cycling / by Libby Wilson.
Description: Chicago: Norwood House Press, 2023 | Series: Trailblazing female athletes | Includes bibliographical references and index. |
Audience: Grades 4-6
Identifiers: LCCN 2022018938 (print) | LCCN 2022018939 (ebook) | ISBN 9781684507566 (hardcover) | ISBN 9781684047994 (paperback) | ISBN 9781684048052 (ebook)
Subjects: LCSH: Women cyclists--Biography--Juvenile literature. | Cycling for women--Juvenile literature. | Cycling--History--Juvenile literature. | Burton, Beryl, 1937---Juvenile literature. | Bicycle racing--History--Juvenile literature.
Classification: LCC GV1051.A1 W56 2023 (print) | LCC GV1051.A1 (ebook) | DDC 796.6082--dc23/eng/20220422
LC record available at https://lccn.loc.gov/2022018938
LC ebook record available at https://lccn.loc.gov/2022018939

Hardcover ISBN: 978-1-68450-756-6
Paperback ISBN: 978-1-68404-799-4

353N—082022
Manufactured in the United States of America in North Mankato, Minnesota.

CONTENTS

FIGHTING FOR THE RIGHT TO RIDE

Women were discouraged from cycling when modern bikes were invented around 1885. At the time, women didn't have the same rights as men. They were expected to stay in the home. Women weren't even allowed to walk down the street alone. Most people were not ready for independent women who rode where they pleased. Some female cyclists were pelted with stones.

Most clothing for women was not bicycle-friendly. Tight corsets pinched their middles to make their waists look tiny. That made it hard to breathe. Long skirts got caught in chains and caused accidents.

Two women ride bicycles in New York's Central Park in 1896.

Women cycled anyway. They rode in pants, a shocking move at the time. However, their riding options were limited. Biking clubs and racetracks outlawed women. They also banned people of color. This segregation created extra barriers for female cyclists of color.

In the 1890s, biking became a craze. Men and women alike rode for fun. Some female cyclists also raced. But society mostly ignored them. Records for men's races date back to 1893. Records for women's races weren't kept until 1955. Men's road racing has been held at every Olympics since 1928. The first Olympic women's road race took place in 1984.

Trailblazing women raced even though opportunities were limited. Because of their achievements, the sport grew. Today, women compete in all kinds of cycling races, whether on roads, tracks, or off-road trails. The top racers also belong to professional cycling teams.

Cycling history abounds with female trailblazers. Kittie Knox not only was one of the sport's early stars but did so as a Black woman during a time of much **discrimination**. Englishwoman Beryl Burton won close to 100 national championships and seven world titles. Juliana Buhring became the first woman to cycle the globe. Olympic champion Marianne Vos promoted women's professional cycling opportunities. Oksana Masters, a double amputee, raised the level of Para-cycling through her many achievements.

Women's cycling has become a popular event at the Olympic Games.

Each of these trailblazers faced incredible obstacles. But their fierce determination brought them success. Giving up was not an option.

CHAPTER ONE

KITTIE KNOX

In 1890, Kittie Knox sailed across the finish line of a 100-mile (161 km) race. Exhilarated, she wiped sweat from her face. As usual, the 16-year-old from Boston, Massachusetts, was among the top finishers. Her companions—white men, mostly—accepted her as part of the group. However, most everybody else tried to keep Knox from biking.

Knox was a Black woman. In her day, "No Women" and "Whites Only" were common racing policies. Knox pushed back against the rules every chance she got.

Knox was known as a scorcher. Scorchers rode fast and hard. This was shocking behavior for a woman. Knox lived during

Kittie Knox defied racial and gender norms as a Black woman who joined a cycling club.

the Victorian age, when women were expected to look and act in a "ladylike" fashion.

Some doctors claimed scorching could harm women's bodies. Doctors warned scorching might prevent women

KITTY KNOX, THE WOMAN SCORCHER.

Kittie Knox was famous for being a scorcher.

QUICK FACT

Knox had the support of much of Boston's cycling leadership and her cycling group. They believed in a Black woman's right to cycle. That was uncommon in the 1890s.

from having babies. Many people thought Victorian tricycles were a more ladylike choice.

Knox kept scorching. But she couldn't scorch in Victorian clothes. Long dresses got tangled in bike chains. Knox found a solution. She was a seamstress. She sewed a cycling outfit with knickerbockers. These were short, wide knee pants. She wore them with a jacket and knee-high boots.

Many people were appalled to see a woman wearing pants.

One woman wrote to a newspaper in 1893 pleading for outfits like Knox's to be illegal. In 1895, Knox entered a contest for the best cycling outfit. She and four white women rode around a large racetrack to display their clothing.

The judges declared Knox the winner. Hissing came from the stands. Was it because of her knickerbockers? Or her skin color? Newspaper reports differed. Still, it was astounding that a Black woman wearing pants was declared better dressed than white women in dresses.

Knox Stands Up to the LAW

QUICK FACT //////

During Knox's time, women often wore up to 12 pounds (5.4 kg) of undergarments with their long dresses. That made biking difficult.

In 1893, Knox joined a national cycling club called the League of the American Wheelmen (LAW). The next year, members from the southern United States demanded that people of color be excluded from the club. When the LAW adopted the rule, many northern clubs ignored it.

In 1895, Knox attended the club's national event in Asbury Park, New Jersey. The event would include rides, races, and a dance. Knox knew her presence might cause problems. But she was going to challenge the ban on Black riders.

An uproar occurred when Knox tried to register. National newspapers included varying reports of what happened. Some said Knox was refused entry. Some said she was upset and was about to leave. A cycling magazine said the LAW's vice president stood by Knox. He discouraged anyone who questioned her club privileges. Knox stayed. Some people were unkind. Others were friendly. She was the only Black person present.

High-Wheel Racer

Louise Armaindo raced **penny-farthing** bikes from 1881 to 1893. Armaindo raced against men, beating most of them. She set a record by riding 600 miles (966 km) in six days. Penny-farthing bikes were unsteady and dangerous. When safer bikes like Knox's were invented, most people stopped riding high-wheelers.

Because of segregation, Knox couldn't use the same hotel or restaurants as the white attendees. But she rode with league members through several towns. They honored Knox by making her the lead rider. During an 18-mile (29 km) race, Knox finished in the top group. Afterward, league members treated her as a star.

A woman in vintage costume poses with a penny-farthing bicycle.

This was not true at the dance, however. Knox's presence upset dozens of white women. They left. But Knox got the last laugh. She stayed and danced all night.

Later, the LAW was asked if Knox was still a member. In its bulletin, it said Knox joined in 1893. The color ban began

Kittie Knox's headstone was finally placed years after her death.

in 1894. The LAW said the rule only applied after 1894. Knox remained a member.

Knox stood up to injustice. Her resistance publicized the unfairness of discrimination. Knox's **perseverance** helped open the doors of cycling for women of all races.

Remembering Kittie Knox

For more than a century, Knox's remains laid in an unmarked grave in Cambridge, Massachusetts. In 2013, the city dedicated a memorial to her with a new headstone. In addition, the Kittie Knox Bike Path opened in 2019. In 2020, the League of American Bicyclists presented its first Kittie Knox Award. It went to Ayesha McGowan, the first Black female pro racer in the United States.

CHAPTER TWO

BERYL BURTON

One morning in 1952, Beryl Charnock pounded her pedals. Sweat streamed beneath her short curls. But it was no use. The 15-year-old couldn't keep up with her cycling club on steep climbs. Her friend, Charlie Burton, pushed her up the hills of Yorkshire, England, all day.

The next week, Beryl showed up for the club ride again. It went no better. But there was no talk of her quitting. She would not be defeated.

According to Charlie, he pushed Beryl up the hills that first year. In her second year, Beryl kept up with the group. By the third year, she was out in front leading the pack.

All of their bike rides brought them close together. Charlie and Beryl married

15

Beryl Burton was one of the most decorated cyclists in racing history.

in 1955. A year later they had their first child. Charlie added a sidecar to his bike, and they continued training.

Beryl Burton was determined to make her mark on the world. She worked 12-hour days as a farm laborer. In the evenings, she pedaled up to 500 miles (805 km) a week while training with an English national cycling champion. Keeping up with him often brought tears to Burton's eyes. But she would not allow herself to drop behind.

A Phenomenal Cycling Career

Burton won her first national bike race in 1957. She then won a silver in her first national 100-mile (161 km) time trial race. In a time trial, the racer who covers a given distance in the shortest time is the winner. In 1959, Burton won her first Britain's Best All-Rounder (B.A.R.) Award. The women's B.A.R. goes to the cyclist with the fastest average speed in the 25-, 50-, and 100-mile (40, 80, and 161 km) races. Burton won the women's B.A.R. 25 years in a row. Nobody else has won more than four times.

In 1959, Burton tried a cycling sport called track pursuit. In pursuit, two riders start on opposite sides of an oval track and race for a given distance. Burton immediately excelled.

Beryl Burton's remarkable stamina allowed her to set records in long-distance competitions.

Burton was invited to the 1959 pursuit world championship in Belgium. There, she beat all competitors to reach the finals. She would ride against the defending champion for the world title.

Burton was nervous. Her hands shook so badly she couldn't feed herself a peeled orange. Charlie had to tie her shoes. But she won, by less than one second. Suddenly, the youngster from Yorkshire was a world champion!

But hardly anyone in Britain noticed. Burton said she might as well have won a local ladies' darts tournament. At that time, women's cycling got little attention from the public.

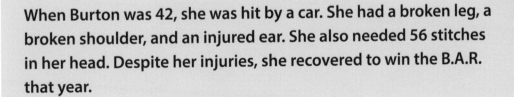

QUICK FACT

Burton won so many races that she lost count of the number. Some experts estimate that she won close to 1,000 races.

Burton's most historic race was a 12-hour time trial in 1967. The race was open to women and men. Over those

Quick Recovery

When Burton was 42, she was hit by a car. She had a broken leg, a broken shoulder, and an injured ear. She also needed 56 stitches in her head. Despite her injuries, she recovered to win the B.A.R. that year.

12 hours, Burton covered 277.25 miles (446.19 km). That was 40 miles (64 km) beyond the previous women's record. It was even 5 miles (8 km) farther than the previous men's record. No woman broke Burton's record for 50 years, despite major advancements in technology that made bikes much faster.

Over the course of her career, Burton brought more attention to the sport of cycling. She also proved that women could be just as competitive as men, and they often could beat them head-to-head if given the chance.

Beryl Burton competes in a race along the English coast.

CHAPTER THREE

JULIANA BUHRING

In July 2012, 31-year-old Juliana Buhring left Naples, Italy, on a bicycle journey around the world. She planned to cover 18,000 miles (29,000 km). By December she had reached the mountains of northern Italy. She had less than 500 miles (805 km) to go to reach the finish line.

However, the temperature was a bone-chilling 16 degrees Fahrenheit (-9°C). Buhring's face was raw with windburn. She had a bloody nose. Two of her toes were black with frostbite. She hoped the damage would be temporary.

Buhring knew warmer weather in southern Italy was only a couple of days away. She was determined to finish her journey. She relied on her strong will to keep pushing. It would help carry her to the finish line.

Juliana Buhring trains for her ride around the world in 2012.

When Buhring reached her final destination of Naples,
a crowd cheered her arrival. Guinness World Records later
recognized her as the fastest woman to bicycle alone around
the world.

Juliana Buhring poses with her bike in Naples, Italy.

Buhring had left Naples on July 23, 2012. She returned on December 22, 2012. In 152 days, she cycled 18,060 miles (29,065 km). Including eight days of rest, that averages out to just over 125 miles (201 km) per day.

Starting from Scratch

Buhring had never ridden a bike until 2011, when she decided to circle the globe. She trained for eight months while looking for **sponsors**. She didn't find any. No one believed a woman who had just begun riding a bike could peddle across the globe. When Buhring was fit enough to average 125 miles a day, she took off anyway.

Buhring's trip was not about seeking adventure. A loved one had died. Buhring had fallen into despair. She went off on the ride seeking an escape from her grief.

Buhring found moments of bliss along the way. In Portugal, she struggled all day to summit a mountain. The exhaustion had her close to tears. Finally, she crested the peak. The thrill of her accomplishment made her grateful to be alive. She called it a rush like no other.

Sometimes, Buhring became bored while she pedaled. She listened to audiobooks to pass the time. At other times, she

Buhring's Bike

On her journey around the world, Buhring rode an ultra-light bike that weighed less than 15 pounds (6.8 kg). A bike shop owner taught her basic repairs. Buhring learned to change tubes, brake pads, and chains. On the road, strangers helped her find parts. During that trip, Buhring's bike suffered 29 tire punctures, eight broken spoke connectors, two broken **derailleurs**, and a broken chain.

was far from bored. In New Zealand, 60-mph (97 kmh) winds blew Buhring off the road. Small birds in Australia repeatedly attacked her face and head. Wild dogs in Turkey gave her the chase of her life. And a brutal stomach virus plagued her throughout India.

But along the way, the kindness of strangers amazed Buhring. People gave her food, drink, and shelter. Anytime she was stopped on the road, it seemed a stranger would pull over to help.

Buhring ran out of money halfway around the world. Fearing she'd have to quit, she posted about her situation online. Soon donations rolled in. Buhring was able to keep going. She had often felt alone in the world, but all the help she received from others made her realize how much support she had.

QUICK FACT

Buhring took a flight to bypass Pakistan, Afghanistan, and Iran on her journey. Women are prohibited or strongly discouraged from cycling in public in these countries.

Juliana Buhring made plenty of friends while cycling around the globe.

Ultra-endurance Racing

After her global trip, Buhring took up ultra-endurance racing. In 2013, she and 30 other bikers raced across Europe. The 2,050-mile (3,300 km) route crossed the towering Alps.

No other woman attempted the race. Buhring rode an average of approximately 170 miles (274 km) per day for 12 days and took ninth place.

In 2014, Buhring was the first woman to finish the Trans Am Bike Race. The 4,322-mile (6,956 km) course across the United States took her 20 days. On day two, Buhring cracked a rib in a crash. But she carried on. Buhring rode the last 36 hours nonstop, covering 500 miles (805 km). She was so exhausted that she needed a wheelchair to board her flight home. It was another example of how hard she pushed herself. Whether traveling alone around the world or taking part in an ultra-endurance race, Buhring showed other female cyclists what was possible with hard work and dedication.

QUICK FACT

Ultra-endurance racers often ride 200 miles (322 km) or more a day during competition. They ride alone, with no help from a support team.

Ultra-endurance racers ride through all kinds of weather and terrain.

CHAPTER FOUR

MARIANNE VOS

During the 2012 Olympic women's road race in London, England, the skies opened up and unleashed a downpour. The wet roads caused one crash after another. Competitors slid into ditches and piled into puddles.

But not Marianne Vos of the Netherlands. She was the world cyclo-cross champion. Cyclo-cross riders battle water and mud in every race. She would win the cyclo-cross world title eight times between 2006 and 2022. No woman in the road race was better prepared to compete in a downpour than Vos.

In the downpour, Vos and Great Britain's Lizzie Deignan escaped the **peloton**. Vos ended the thrilling Olympic race by

Marianne Vos races through the rain during the 2012 Olympic women's road race.

sprinting up the final hill. Deignan followed Vos to the finish, spluttering in Vos's **rooster tail** spray.

G.O.A.T.

Many consider Vos to be the greatest all-around female cyclist of all time. She won world championships in the dirt,

Marianne Vos rejoices after winning the 2012 Olympic women's road race.

on the road, and on the track. She earned two Olympic golds. Plus, she won several international mountain bike events. Few women cyclists have ever been as **versatile**.

The toughest women's road race is the Giro d'Italia Donne. It is contested in stages that take place over several days. In 2012, the race included the 7,523-foot (2,293 m) monster climb into the Italian Alps. Vos won that race three times. She is called the G.O.A.T of the Giro Donne. That means she is the Greatest Of All Time.

Vos's explosive riding drew worldwide attention to her sport. That was exactly what women's cycling needed in 2012. At the time, the sport had few fans and few sponsors. There were too few races and not enough riders. Pay was low. Few women could afford the equipment and travel expenses.

QUICK FACT

There are four types of cycling races in the Olympics. They are BMX, mountain, road, and track.

This was not true in men's cycling. Male cyclists earned much higher salaries. Their events were well-supported. Women wanted equal treatment for their sport.

One problem was that women's cycling was rarely televised. It's hard for fans to follow a sport they can't watch.

Cyclo-cross

Cyclo-cross racers follow a looped course in fields and woods. They race over large roots and through deep ruts. Riders dismount and shoulder their bikes for run-ups. These can include stairs, sand pits, or mud. Racers haul their bikes over streams and wooden barriers. They descend steep, cliff-like hills.

Marianne Vos celebrates after winning the road race at the 2013 World Championships in Italy.

Luckily, Vos's entire Olympic race had been televised. Her ability to climb and sprint to the finish captivated viewers. People wanted to see more of her.

Vos's next race after the Olympics was the road race at that year's World Championships. It was held in the Netherlands, Vos's home country. Vos had won the race in 2006. But she'd come in second the following five years. Vos had grown more frustrated with each silver medal.

Media hyped the upcoming race. Would Vos break her silver streak at home? Would Deignan avenge her Olympic silver?

On race day, Vos sprinted up the last hill to capture gold. She grabbed a fan's flag and waved it as she crossed the finish line. The crowd roared. Vos's popularity soared. So did public interest in women's cycling.

Lizzie Deignan

Lizzie Deignan has won world titles on both the road and the track. Like Vos, she works to improve women's cycling. She fights for riders' rights and better media coverage. Deignan was one of the first mothers in women's pro cycling. She was back racing seven months after giving birth in 2019.

A Champion for Women's Cycling

Vos used her star status to improve her sport. Her dream was to make cycling more accessible and popular for women. Vos worked with leaders of world cycling organizations. She spoke out during media interviews.

Her campaign brought progress. The changes in women's cycling have been incredible, Vos reports. She says the sport is almost unrecognizable from when she started in 2006.

Today, more teams are competing at a world-class level. They travel on buses paid for by their teams. Riders earn better pay. All Women's World Tour races are televised. New sponsors fund longer, harder races. And in 2022 a women's Tour de France was back on the racing calendar for the first time in more than 30 years.

The gap between women's and men's cycling has narrowed. But inequality still exists. Vos has vowed to continue her determined effort to create opportunities for women cyclists.

Marianne Vos played a big role in increasing the popularity of women's cycling around the world.

CHAPTER FIVE

OKSANA MASTERS

The starting signal buzzed for the time trial at the **Paralympic Games** in 2021. Oksana Masters powered her handcycle around the racetrack in Tokyo, Japan. The 32-year-old Masters listened for her coach's voice in her earpiece. Coaches monitor competitors' time and give technical advice. But the audio equipment had failed. Masters was on her own.

To stay calm, Masters focused on deep breathing. She repeatedly counted to ten. With her mind busy, her body took over. Masters stayed focused the entire 15-mile (24 km) course.

Masters crossed the finish line 45 minutes later, exhausted. She screamed in joy and disbelief when she learned that she'd

Oksana Masters celebrates after winning the road race at the 2021 Paralympic Games.

won gold. Surely, she was dreaming. But no, this was her dream come true.

Transformed by Sports

Masters had come far, from a child in a Ukrainian orphanage to a powerful Paralympic champion. She was born in 1989

Oksana Masters adjusts her prostheses while training for the rowing competition at her first Paralympics in London, England.

with many birth defects. One leg was 6 inches (15 cm) longer than the other. She had no shin bones or thumbs. She had just one kidney, and part of her stomach was missing.

An American woman, Gay Masters, adopted Oksana at age seven. In the United States, Oksana endured many operations. Doctors amputated both legs. They used a series of surgeries to create thumbs for her.

At age 13, Masters began **adaptive** rowing. Athletics transformed her life. She felt a new sense of freedom and purpose. The workouts helped banish the trauma of her past.

Masters trained hard for ten years. In 2012, she qualified for her first Paralympics.

By 2014, Masters had won Paralympic medals in rowing and seated cross-country skiing. She took up handcycling in 2014 after an injury ended her rowing career. She loved cycling's speed. She could go much faster than in her other sports.

In 2016, Masters qualified for the US Paralympic cycling team. But her races at the Rio Games didn't go well. Her aluminum bike was heavy and slow. Her handgrips were ill-fitted. Masters left Brazil without a medal. She was determined to do better in the 2020 Paralympics.

Masters began training six to eight hours a day. Workouts included weight lifting, aerobic conditioning, and riding. Masters won two silver

QUICK FACT

Toyota became a Paralympic sponsor. The company built Masters a fast, lightweight carbon bike. Toyota also custom-fitted her handgrips. The changes helped her cycling performance.

medals in the 2019 World Championships. She was ready to go for gold at the Paralympic Games in Tokyo. But she had to wait, as the Tokyo Games were delayed by a year due to the COVID-19 pandemic.

Health Scare

About three months before she was to leave for Tokyo in 2021, Masters experienced agonizing leg pain. She was terrified. Doctors operated and removed a large tumor.

Masters wondered if she would be able to continue her training. She thought of her years of hard work. She might not have a chance to add to her legacy. She had never felt lower.

Masters worked hard to make a comeback. Winning a gold medal was no longer the goal. She just wanted to make the team that would compete in Tokyo.

Oksana Masters competes in cross-country skiing at the 2014 Winter Paralympic Games in Sochi, Russia.

But Masters crashed in the US Paralympic team trials. Fortunately, she had proven herself in other competitions. Because of that, she was still selected for the team.

In Tokyo, Masters shocked herself by winning gold in the time trial. Two days later, she won a second gold in the road race. Masters won easily, finishing three minutes before the silver medalist.

With her wins, Masters became one of only four women to have won a gold medal in both the Summer and Winter Paralympics. And six months later, she was back at the Winter Paralympics. With seven more medals, she became the most decorated US Winter Paralympian of all time. In total, across her sports Masters had won 17 Paralympic medals and 22 world championship medals. She had raised the bar for all competitors in Para sports.

Versatile Star

Masters also is a Paralympic athlete in Nordic skiing and biathlon. Between the 2016 Summer Games in Rio and the Tokyo Summer Games in 2021, she participated in the 2018 Winter Paralympics in PyeongChang, South Korea. She won five medals there—two golds, two silvers, and a bronze.

CONCLUSION

Cyclists compete in the women's road race at the Tokyo Olympics in 2021.

In the 1890s, women were discouraged from biking. Today, women's cycling is a professional sport. These five inspiring, determined women helped create that change. They were pioneers who broke gender and race barriers. They beat male competitors head-to-head. They proved their strength and courage on long-distance rides through brutal conditions. They overcame physical challenges to shine on the world stage. They will be remembered as trailblazers in women's cycling.

GLOSSARY

adaptive
in sports, modified for people with disabilities

derailleurs
mechanisms on a bike that shift the chain from one gear to another

discrimination
unfair treatment based on characteristics such as gender and race

Paralympic Games
an international multisport competition for athletes with physical disabilities that runs parallel with the Olympics

peloton
the main pack of riders in a bicycle race

penny-farthing
a type of bike with a huge front wheel and a tiny back wheel, named for two English coins

perseverance
continued effort to do something difficult

rooster tail
the gritty water spray from the back wheel of a bike in the rain

sponsors
people or organizations that pay for an activity

versatile
turning with ease from one thing to another

FOR MORE INFORMATION

Books

Fretland VanVoorst, Jenny. *The Science behind Cycling*. Minneapolis, MN: Jump!, 2020.

Herman, Gail. *What Are the Paralympic Games?* New York, NY: Penguin Workshop, 2020.

Hogan, Christa C. *Mountain Biking*. Minneapolis, MN: Abdo, 2019.

Websites

Marianne Vos
mariannevosofficial.com

Get the latest news and results on Vos's official website.

Oksana Masters
oksanamastersusa.com

Read all about the accomplishments of the US Paralympian.

USA Cycling
usacycling.org

USA Cycling is the governing body for bicycle racing—including road, track, mountain bike, cyclo-cross, and BMX—in the United States.

INDEX

ABOUT THE AUTHOR

Libby Wilson is happy on a bicycle. She has biked around Greece, Denmark, and the Florida Keys. Wilson loves to write about people who inspire her. She is a retired librarian and is always surrounded by books. Wilson lives in Saegertown, Pennsylvania, and Charlotte, North Carolina.